Our very

Tony & Denise

Christmas 1979

From:

Garry & Carolyn

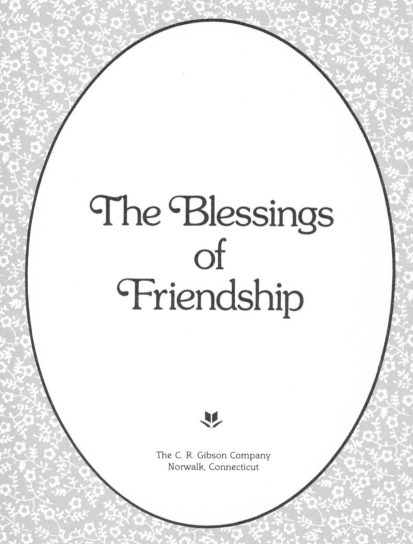

The Blessings
of
Friendship

The C. R. Gibson Company
Norwalk, Connecticut

A faithful friend is a sturdy shelter;
he who finds one finds a treasure.

There is no blood between us, no common family history. Yet there are no barriers of background, or even age. Older, younger, richer, poorer—no matter. We speak the same language, we have come together in a special moment of time. How generous is God that He has given me these men and women I can call friends.

Marjorie Holmes

To a
Friend

You entered my life in a casual way,
And saw at a glance what I needed;
There were others who passed me or met me
   each day,
But never a one of them heeded.
Perhaps you were thinking of other folks more,
Or chance simply seemed to decree it;
I know there were many such chances before,
But the others—well, they didn't see it.

You said just the thing that I wished you would say,
And you made me believe that you meant it;
I held up my head in the old gallant way,
And resolved you should never repent it.
There are times when encouragement means such a lo

And a word is enough to convey it;
There were others who could have, as easy as not—
But, just the same, they didn't say it.

There may have been someone who could have
   done more
To help me along, though I doubt it;
What I needed was cheering, and always before
They had let me plod on without it.
You helped to refashion the dream of my heart,
And made me turn eagerly to it;
There were others who might have (I question that part)—
But, after all, they didn't do it!

Grace Stricker Dawson

Friendship

The glory of friendship is not the outstretched
hand, nor the kindly smile, nor the joy of
companionship; it is the spiritual inspiration that
comes to one when he discovers that someone
believes in him and is willing to trust him with his
friendship.

Ralph Waldo Emerson

The
Things
I Prize

These are the things I prize
And hold of dearest worth:
Light of the sapphire skies,
Peace of the silent hills,
Shelter of the forests, comfort of the grass,
Music of birds, murmurs of little rills,
Shadows of cloud that swiftly pass,
And, after showers,
The smell of flowers
And of the good brown earth,—
And best of all, along the way, friendship and
mirth.

Henry van Dyke

A Prayer

It is my joy in life to find
At every turning of the road,
The strong arm of a comrade kind
To help me onward with my load.

And since I have no gold to give,
And love alone must make amends,
My only prayer is, while I live,—
God make me worthy of my friends!

Frank Dempster Sherman

A faithful friend is a sturdy shelter;
he who finds one finds a treasure.
A faithful friend is beyond price,
no sum can balance his worth.
A faithful friend is a life-saving remedy,
such as he who fears God finds;
For he who fears God behaves accordingly,
and his friend will be like himself.

Ecclesiasticus 6:14-17

To
My
Friend

I love you not only for what you are, but for what I
am when I am with you.

I love you not only for what you have made of
yourself, but for what you are making of me.

I love you because you have done more than any
creed could have done to make me good, and
more than any fate could have done to make me
happy.

You have done it without a touch, without a word,
without a sign.

You have done it by being yourself. Perhaps that is
what being a friend means, after all.

Roy Croft

The Rarest Faith

Friendship takes place between those who have an affinity for one another, and is a perfectly natural and inevitable result. No professions or advances will avail. Even speech, at first, necessarily has nothing to do with it; but it follows after silence, as the buds in the graft do not put forth into leaves till long after the graft has taken. It is a drama in which the parties have no part to act. . . .

Friendship is never established as an understood relation. Do you demand that I be less your friend that you may know it? Yet what right have I to think that another cherishes so rare a sentiment for me? It is a miracle which requires constant proofs. It is an exercise of the finest imagination and the rarest faith. It says by a silent but eloquent behavior: "I will be so related to thee as thou canst not imagine; even so thou mayest believe. I will spend truth, all my wealth on thee," and the friend responds silently through his nature, and life, and treats his friend with the same divine courtesy. . . .

The language of Friendship is not words but meaning. It is an intelligence above language. One imagines endless conversations with his friend, in which the tongue shall be loosed, and thoughts be spoken, without hesitancy, or end; but the experience is commonly far otherwise. . . .

Suppose you go to bid farewell to your friend who is setting out on a journey; what other outward sign do you know than to shake his hand . . . ? There are some things which a man never speaks of, which are much finer kept silent about. To the highest communications we only lend a silent ear. . . . In human intercourse the tragedy begins, not when there is misunderstanding about words, but when silence is not understood.

Henry David Thoreau

There are friends who pretend to be friends, but there is a friend who sticks closer than a brother.

Proverbs 18:24

Definition

True friendship comes when silence between two people is comfortable.

Dave Tyson Gentry

Friendship is an arrangement by which we undertake to exchange small favors for big ones.

Baron de Montesquieu

True friendship is like sound health, the value of it is seldom known until it be lost.

Charles Caleb Colton

One's friends are that part of the human race with which one can be human.

George Santayana

Friendship

And a youth said, "Speak to us of Friendship."
    And he answered, saying:
    "Your friend is your needs answered.
    He is your field which you sow with love and
reap with thanksgiving.
    And he is your board and your fireside.
    For you come to him with your hunger, and you
seek him for peace.

    "When your friend speaks his mind you fear not
the 'nay' in your own mind, nor do you withhold
the 'ay.'
    And when he is silent, your heart ceases not to
listen to his heart;
    For without words, in friendship, all thoughts,
all desires, all expectations are born and shared,
with joy that is unacclaimed.

When you part from your friend, you grieve not;

For that which you love most in him may be clearer in his absence, as the mountain to the climber is clearer from the plain.

"And let there be no purpose in friendship save the deepening of the spirit.

For love that seeks aught but the disclosure of its own mystery is not love but a net cast forth: and only the unprofitable is caught.

"And let your best be for your friend.

If he must know the ebb of your tide, let him know its flood also.

For what is your friend that you should seek him with hours to kill?

Seek him always with hours to live.

For it is his to fill your need, but not your emptiness.

And in the sweetness of friendship let there be laughter, and sharing of pleasures.

For in the dew of little things the heart finds its morning and is refreshed."

Kahlil Gibran

Friendship

Oh, the comfort—the inexpressible comfort
of feeling safe with a person,
Having neither to weigh thoughts,
Nor measure words—but pouring them
All right out—just as they are—
Chaff and grain together—
Certain that a faithful hand will
Take and sift them—
Keep what is worth keeping—
And with the breath of kindness
Blow the rest away.

Dinah Maria Mulock Craik

It
Takes
Two

The desire for friendship is strong in every human heart. We crave the companionship of those who understand. The nostalgia of life presses, we sigh for "home," and long for the presence of one who sympathizes with our aspirations, comprehends our hopes, and is able to partake of our joys. A thought is not our own until we impart it to another, and the confessional seems to be a crying need of every human soul.

One can bear grief, but it takes two to be glad.

Elbert Hubbard

A
Time
to Talk

When a friend calls to me from the road
And slows his horse to a meaning walk,
I don't stand still and look around
On all the hills I haven't hoed,
And shout from where I am, "What is it?"
No, not as there is a time to talk.
I thrust my hoe in the mellow ground,
Blade-end up and five feet tall,
And plod: I go up to the stone wall
For a friendly visit.

Robert Frost

The Art of Friendship

The first step in the art of friendship is to be a friend; then making friends takes care of itself. To be a friend a man should start by being a friend to himself, by being true to his highest and best and by aligning himself with the enduring values of human life that make for growth and progress.

To be a friend a man should strive to be "like the shadow of a great rock in a weary land," to be a source of refuge and strength to those who walk in darkness.

To be a friend a man should believe in the inherent goodness of men and in their potential greatness; he should treat men in a big spirit, expectant of a noble response.

To be a friend a man should strive to lift people up, not cast them down; to encourage, not discourage; to set an example that will be an inspiration to others.

To be a friend a man should be sensitively responsive to the dreams and aims of others and should show sincere appreciation for the contributions others make to the enrichment of his life.

To be a friend a man should practice the companionship of silence and the magic of words that his speech may build and not destroy, help and not hinder.

To be a friend a man should close his eyes to the faults of others and open them to his own.

To be a friend a man should not attempt to reform or reprimand, but should strive only to make others happy if he can.

To be a friend a man should be himself, he should be done with hypocrisy, artificiality and pretense, he should meet and mingle with people in quiet simplicity and humility.

To be a friend a man should be tolerant, he should have an understanding heart and a forgiving nature, knowing that all men stumble now and then, and that he who never made a mistake never accomplished anything.

To be a friend a man should join hands with all people who are working for great principles, great purposes and great causes; he should put his shoulder to the wheel to help achieve common goals.

To be a friend a man should go more than halfway with his fellow men; he should greet others first and not wait to be greeted; he should radiate a spirit of overflowing good will.

To be a friend a man should remember that we are human magnets; that like attracts like, and that what we give we get.

To be a friend a man should recognize that no man knows all the answers, and that he should add each day to his knowledge of how to live the friendly way.

Wilferd A. Peterson

Thank You for Being a Friend

Thank you for being a friend to me when needing someone there—my failing hopes to bolster and my secret fears to share . . . Thank you for being so good to me when it was hard to know—the wisest course to follow, what to do and where to go.

Thank you for giving me confidence when I had lost my way—speaking the word that led me through the tunnel of the day . . . Thank you for all you did and said to ease the weight for me—Never intruding, but there in the background, helping quietly.

Thank you not only for sympathy in times of grief and stress—but for all you have meant to me in terms of happiness . . . Many a lovely day we've known and many a laugh we've had—Thank you for being the kind of friend that shares the good and bad.

Patience Strong

Two are better than one, because they have a good reward for their toil. For if they fall, one will lift up his fellow; but woe to him who is alone when he falls and has not another to lift him up. Again, if two lie together, they are warm; but how can one be warm alone? And though a man might prevail against one who is alone, two will withstand him. A threefold cord is not quickly broken.

Ecclesiastes 4:9-12

Friends can be friends for many reasons: the neighbor willing to help; the wit who makes you laugh; the quiet one who sometimes startles you with a gem of philosophy. How lovely—this variety. That all our friends needn't be alike! Friendships can be infinitely varied. By their differentness, the whole pattern of one's days can be enriched. Sift through your friendships; sort them. There is the rich inner circle of those people who are dearest to your heart. These are the persons to whom we can most honestly express our deepest selves. And even though we may not see them for days, weeks—even years—the bond remains strong and true.

Marjorie Holmes

Being with people you like and respect is so meaningful. Perhaps you have known some of them most of your life. Having friends around for a pleasant evening is one of life's most cherished joys as far as I am concerned. But when those with me are fellow believers how much greater that joy is, for we know that it will be rekindled, one day, in eternity.

James Stewart

The greatest joy life can hold for any man is the pleasure of giving. I like to see people smile and laugh and feel happy.

Lawrence Welk

I very firmly believe . . . that I've never met a stranger.

Doris Day

Good Neighbors, Good Friends

Friendship means sharing interests and this means widening one's horizon. It involves loving kindness and patience, never faultfinding or criticism. Too often I hear people explaining just what their friends have done wrong. I do not consider this true friendship!

. . . My own dearest friends seem neither to have faults themselves nor to find them in others. They seem always to be giving generously of themselves, without question or pause, and even the smallest of incidents will remind me of this.

For example, there are my nearest neighbors, Kay and Pret, who live in a house next to mine on Mill Pond. I remember a short time ago when I was trying to start my car and it made a lot of noise but would not move an inch. Before I could get out, Pret came rushing down the road.

"Sounds as if you are having trouble," Pret said.
I made my appointment on time!
Pret is a champion fisherman and I may come home from town to find a bagful of freshly dug clams or some flounder fillets while Kay pops in with a bouquet of their elegant garden flowers or some new peas and fresh lettuce. Being a good neighbor is an art which makes life richer.

Gladys Taber

A true friend is one soul in two bodies.

Aristotle

He who withholds kindness from a friend forsakes the fear of the Almighty.

Job 6:14

I have three chairs
in my house: one for solitude,
two for friendship, three for company.

Henry David Thoreau

New Friends and Old Friends

Make new friends, but keep the old;
Those are silver, these are gold.
New-made friendships, like new wine,
Age will mellow and refine.
Friendships that have stood the test—
Time and change—are surely best;
Brow may wrinkle, hair grow gray;
Friendship never knows decay.
For 'mid old friends, tried and true,
Once more we our youth renew.
But old friends, alas! may die;
New friends must their place supply.
Cherish friendship in your breast—
New is good, but old is best;
Make new friends, but keep the old;
Those are silver, these are gold.

Joseph Parry

What Is a Friend?

What is a friend? I will tell you. It is a person with whom you dare to be yourself. Your soul can be naked with him. He seems to ask of you to put on nothing, only to be what you are. He does not want you to be better or worse. You do not have to be on your guard. You can say what you think, so long as it is genuinely you. He understands those contradictions in your nature that lead others to misjudge you. With him you breathe freely. He understands. You do not have to be careful. You can abuse him, neglect him, tolerate him. Best of all, you can keep still with him. It makes no matter. He likes you. He is like fire that purges to the bone. He understands. He understands. You can weep with him, laugh with him, pray with him. Through it all—and underneath—he sees, knows and loves you. A friend? What is a friend? Just one, I repeat, with whom you dare to be yourself.

Raymond Beran

Friendship's Growth

Friendships do not grow up in any carefully tended and contemplated fashion. . . . They begin haphazard.

As we look back on the first time we saw our friends we find that generally our original impression was curiously astray. We have worked along beside them, have grown to cherish their delicious absurdities, have outrageously imposed on each other's patience—and suddenly we awoke to realize what had happened.

We had, without knowing it, gained a new friend. In some curious way the unseen border line had been passed. We had reached the final culmination of Anglo-Saxon regard when two men rarely look each other straight in the eyes because they are ashamed to show each other how fond they are.

We had reached the fine flower and the ultimate test of comradeship—that is, when you get a letter from one of your best friends, you know you don't need to answer it until you get ready to.

Christopher Morley

Friends

    Friends are like the sturdy oaks that rustle in the
breeze when the summer suns are gone . . . Like
the boughs of spicy evergreens pressed against
our lives to shelter from the wintry blast . . .
Friends are like low blooming flowers that break at
spring to light our path . . . Like the perfumed
roses dropping petals of happiness around our
door . . . Friends are like green mosses clinging
close to running brooks . . . Like the flowing
streams spreading their moisture along the fields
and asking no reward or pay . . . Friends are like
the shady nooks giving sweet release at evening's
hush . . . Like the broad expanse of softest green
and copper bronze to delight the eye . . . Friends
are like the gentle whisperings of a love divine . . .
Forgiving and forgetting without a tinge of blame.

Bertha Keiningham

Acknowledgments

The editor and the publisher have made every effort to trace the ownership of all copyrighted material and to secure permission from copyright holders of such material. In the event of any question arising as to the use of any material the publisher and editor, while expressing regret for inadvertent error, will be pleased to make the necessary corrections in future printings. Thanks are due to the following authors, publishers, publications and agents for permission to use the material indicated.

Selected by Patricia Dreier

Designed by Bonnie Weber

Set in Italia Light
and Souvenir Light Swash

Photo Credits